Out of the Labyrinth

Previous book by Nanne Nyander
Silence. Angels and Poems (2018)

Title: Out of the Labyrinth. Poems
© Nanne Nyander 2022.
www.nannenyander.se
Published by: BoD – Books on Demand, Stockholm, Sverige
Printed by: BoD – Books on Demand, Norderstedt, Tyskland
Cover, book design and drawing by Nanne Nyander.
ISBN: 978-91-8027-975-8

Get Out of the Labyrinth!

Requiem for my ego.

1.

I will sing to you,
my precious one.
Will you listen?
Are you ready?
I'm your guide,
I'm your angel,
guiding you out of this darkness.
The darkness seems daunting,
but the dark cannot live where there is light.
Can you see the light?
I will take you there,
just follow the signs.
I'll keep singing till you see the light,
I'll sing till you wake up.
I'll sing you a song,
about I.

2.

I walk alone,
blindfolded through the glory of life.
I walk alone.
How could it be missed?
This reality of mine is just an illusion.
The truth is staring me in the face,
yet, I walk alone,
blindfolded through the misery of life.
What is real and what is not?
The question keeps coming back to me,
as I walk alone, blindfolded,
with my hands tied behind my back.
Untie me,
and I will pull back the veil,
take off the blindfold,
and I'll be home,
walking with my eyes wide open
through the glory of life.

3.

Be innocent, but not too innocent.

4.

No separation,
no touch to be found.
Why?
We are one.
I can touch your heart, your heart is mine.
I can feel your feelings, as they too were mine.
They are not mine,
they are not even yours.
They are just feelings.
Still, they overwhelm me
to the point that I don't know who I am.
No separation,
only I can be found.

5.

Inside of me is a space where I can hide,
hide from my mind and everything it's telling me.
Here I can be alive.
Here I can be myself.
Connect the infinite with the infinite,
let there be no gap in the fabric of grace.

6.

Loud is the noise in my head,
loud and entangled in itself.
Without a map showing me how to get out,
I am stuck.
As soon as I find a way,
there is another obstacle in front of me
that I haven't seen before,
and I'm in it, forgetting what I was doing.
Wandering around like a zombie again,
I thought I was almost there,
I could see the way out,
or could I?
I can't tell anymore.
I know I was on my way out.
What am I doing here?
I can see the exit.
The noise rearranges everything,
and again, I'm lost.
How long can I keep this up?
Mind is like a labyrinth
in which I thought I knew the way out.
I don't remember ever being told
that it would be so hard.
Mind is not like a labyrinth, it's like a maze,
I have no clue how to get out of this chaotic landscape
that I have created for myself.

I lie down and give up,
let me just lie here and decompose,
turn into daffodils.
Nothing can touch me now,
because I am nothing.
I am Nothing, I always was.
How can nothing be lost?
I guess nothing was lost,
and now it is found.

7.

I am perfect just as I am, but what am I?

8.

I'm gasping for air, hold me tight,
I'm losing myself completely,
losing myself to myself.
No more unconscious postponing.
No postponing possible.
Nowhere to run,
nowhere to go.
I'm nowhere to be found,
I'm now here to be found.
I'm now here!
I'm here.
I AM.

9.

In an insane world,
who is the winner?
The insane person,
or the one who has left it all behind,
the one who has realised she is nothing?
In an insane world,
what is the goal?
To become more insane
or to realise you're the one watching it all passing by?
In an insane world,
are you the participator or the spectator?
Or are you both?

10.

Thoughts are like leaves in the autumn,
don't get attached to them,
let them do their dance,
let them do their intriguing dance and move on.

11.

Save nothing,
leave everything behind,
don't salvage anything,
become empty.
Enter nothing with nothing.

12.

Looking fear in the eyes,
we stare at each other for a lifetime.
All my life,
I have stared fear in the face,
I only now realise,
fear wasn't real,
fear wasn't fear,
fear was just my own reflection in the mirror.

13.

It's a bird in my heart,
singing for freedom,
freedom from self.
It's a bird in my heart desperately trying to get out.
I open my heart and let it in.

14.

I lose myself in the infinite,
I can feel the fear of losing my mind,
the fear is there even though I want to lose it,
my mind, my ego, the chatter in my head.
Mind is luring me
to keep my attention on its dressed up garbage.
How can it still be so enticing?
But yet I let go,
I let go into the infinite,
I have been avoiding nirvana without even knowing it.

15.

You talk to me seldom,
or is it me not listening,
too occupied with all the nonsense in my head,
not knowing when it's you speaking.
Once in a while,
I can hear you trying to guide me,
I do my best to understand,
and then I get lost again,
lost in the dreamlike insane non-reality
that is occupying the space where thoughts travel.
Talk to me,
this time I will listen.

16.

Lost in the forest of one's mind.
Walk deeper into the forest and lose yourself.
Come back empty.
Stay empty,
stay out of reach of the gravitation of the mind.

17.

Here I can watch myself
trying to get out of the labyrinth of my mind's creation.
I can see myself crying and screaming on the inside
and smiling on the outside.
But I'm neither of these.
Now I'm calm and still, watching my thoughts,
but I can see that too.
Now I'm lost in meaningless mind-babble.
It feels more sticky and foggy,
but I can still see it.
Can you?
Sometimes the fog is so thick that I get lost in it.
I'm so afraid of not finding my way back home.
But why?
I'm here watching that too.

18.

Memories are flowing by,
like a boring movie,
which I have already seen a hundred times.
When will this end?
Am I dying?
I guess, in a way,
I'm dying, bit by bit.
What I am not, is dying in front of my eyes,
shredding memories of this life,
getting lighter,
thinner till it one day will evaporate into thin air,
be recomposed into something more beautiful,
more magnificent,
more nothing.
Sweet, beautiful nothing.

19.

Empty world, empty words.
Everyone is talking, but no one is listening.

20.

Music is going through my body.
Music is energy,
my body is energy,
my body is moving to the music without moving.
I'm still,
everything is still,
inside me,
outside of me.
I hear a distant drum,
a silent sound from a distant life,
a life long gone,
urging me to let go.
"Hold on no more."
The music hits every particle of my body.
I am the music,
I'm energy,
I am life.
I'm everything.
I am nothing.
I am.
I AM.

21.

Prepare yourself for the ride of your life,
a rollercoaster you could never have imagined.
It will scare you,
it will make you cry,
it will make you scream,
"let me off this ride,"
but it's too late.
This rollercoaster is your life.

22.

Remembering a time without time.
I'm swimming in the void of nothingness.
Lose yourself with me,
We are all free to dance our own dance.
Empty yourself from all beliefs.
We are not of this world,
we are just here for now.
Patience, my dear friend!
Sweet nothingness.
Stay where there are no thoughts,
stay in the void where nothing can disturb you.
Stay as I am, as I,
as nothing, as everything.
This is just the beginning of the end.

23.

Hurry up to slow down.

24.

Victory is near,
pain is here,
you are present as I walk into the fire
that washes all the spiderwebs away from my eyes.
I can see you.
Can you see me?
Can you see me through the fog that covers your eyes?
I strip my identity away,
I'm losing my ego.
Don't pick it up for me.
Don't help me to build a new one.
Let me stay empty.
Don't try to find me.
I'm gone, let me be gone.
I'm empty, let me be empty.
I'm dead, let me be dead.
Walk beside me, walk with me,
walk with me as one.
Let us be unidentified.
Let us be Awake.

25.

Wake up! WAKE UP!

26.

Fear nothing,
I'm here,
I'll walk with you,
but you have to wake up alone.
It's a path in the forest,
which is no path,
a path to nowhere,
stay on it,
walk no more,
you're already here.
Just stay.
Can you see me?
Can you hear me?
I'm here, my beloved.
I'm here,
Awake,
going nowhere.
And so are you.

27.

My world is falling apart.
The dream doesn't hold together anymore.
I'm losing interest in the illusion,
in the gravitational pull of thought.

28.

Everything is muddy,
my feet are stuck to the ground,
the clouds are big and dark,
but I fear nothing,
the clouds bring the rain,
the rain pours over me,
over my face and washes my tears away,
washes all the mud away,
I'm free,
I can see clearly now,
I no longer fear nothing.

29.

I'm here, I'm done.
This is the beginning of my freedom.
Precious memories
of a beautiful past that never happened.
What is it I tell myself to keep believing in these lies,
all these lies that the mind keeps telling me?
I just listen and don't take much interest in
what it tells me anymore.
I can see its desperate attempts to lure me in.
I don't want to play that game.
I stay at a distance and just watch.
It tells me the most amazing things,
but I can't believe them anymore.
Sometimes it succeeds, and I do what it tells me to do,
all to distract me from I.
But I don't want to be distracted anymore.
It's all unbelievably crazy.
I'm here. I am.

30.

The shadows of the night,
cloud my judgement.
I'm stuck in this quicksand,
going everywhere,
when I need to go nowhere,
nowhere feels impossible in this murky water.
I feel no fear,
even though every move pulls me
further down into oblivion.
"Do nothing!" I can hear you say.
I'm trying.
"Don't try.
You can't try, to do nothing,
that's doing something,
and you will be stuck forever."
I have been swimming my whole life,
trying to keep my head above water.
It's time to let go.
No one can save me now.
Oblivion is my companion,
as welcome as a lifebuoy made out of concrete.
"Stop treading water,
it makes the water murky.
Be still, do nothing."
The water clears up,
It's shallow,
I can stand here without disturbing
the clear water of the ever-present truth.
The truth that I am.

31.

I stand before you,
when all becomes one, and one becomes all.
I'm here for you and for me,
when everything becomes nothing
and nothing becomes everything.

32.

Lost in the struggle with the mind.
Insignificant noise within the immense silence,
the eternal light of the one.

33.

The realisation hits me,
I'm following my own shadow.
The self is nowhere to be found
when you let the light in.

34.

Behind those clouds of yours, what can you see?
Behind those words of yours, what do you mean?
Behind that face of yours, what do you feel?
If you ignore the clouds, skip the words,
and stop hiding behind your mask.
What do you see?
Everything is clear behind the clouds.
Everything makes sense without the words.
Your face can tell the truth,
if you want to.
Leave the world of duality for now,
and enter this world as you are,
as You are without you.

35.

Echoes of my own distant voice hit my ears.
Wake up!

36.

I'm here.
No need to go anywhere.
I feel everything is pulling me in all directions.
No need to leave.
No need to give in.
Just stay, watch, and be.

37.

I'm going insane,
I'm losing myself,
or am I just losing the part of me
that isn't the truth of what I am?
I'm like a snake who's shedding its skin,
I'm leaving it all behind.
Or am I like the caterpillar
that is turning into a butterfly,
suffocating in its cocoon?
How long do I have to stay in here?
There is no me,
no snake,
no caterpillar,
no cocoon.
It's all in my head,
which is not even my head,
I'm stuck in a movie that is not even real.

38.

Waves of music flow through my body,
anchor in my heart.
The music carries me away,
far away from the entanglement of thoughts.
My body touches the wet grass,
feeling the air beneath me,
around me.
The music takes me to the top of the mountain.
Here I can see everything clearly,
the view is spectacular.
I can see every thought,
every memory,
the pain,
the hope,
the despair.
I'm only watching,
I can see everything for what it is.
My beautifully distorted world.

39.

Stop looking for me, and you will find me.
I'm waiting for you, but not waiting.
I'm here, where you are, always.
Searching is an obstacle to finding me.
See that you are already here, resting in my arms,
together we're watching the universe go by.
You and I are one.
You're one with me, one with the universe.
It's all one.
That's why you can't find me.
I'm here watching you running around
thinking you are someone,
someone separate from me.
You and I will never be separate.
Rest in my arms, stay with me.
Remember who you are,
and just stay with me, my love.

40.

Lost in the woods,
I run and run, no time to stop.
Desperately looking for the way home.
Finely I get so exhausted that I fall down,
lying on my back, looking up at the sky,
looking all around me,
too tired to do anything,
too tired to move.
I suddenly realise,
I AM home.
I have been running around in circles.
I have been here the whole time,
just thinking I was lost.

41.

Wake up!
Go to the horizon of your mind.
Do not pass me by.
Look at me like you once did.
Don't you see me?
How long are you going to look for me this time?
Relax.
Do not search for me where you think you can find me.
The summer wind is stroking your cheek.
I am stroking your cheek,
you are not really here,
you are the summer wind,
you are me.

42.

I'm an alien to you,
I'm an alien to me,
I have no idea what is going on in this human entity.
Watch me disappear into thin air,
I know you can see me, but I'm not really here.
I'm watching you, watching me.
I'm watching me, watching you.
I can see my mind spinning like a circus act in hell.
No need to watch,
no need to follow,
no need to see the end,
I have seen it before. It's a rerun.
I can see you're watching me.
I'm an alien to you.
I'm an alien to me.
I don't really exist.

43.

From where I stand,
I can see everything,
I perceive everything, I feel everything,
but nothing can touch me.
From where I stand,
I'm nothing,
I'm nobody,
From where I stand,
I suffer no more.

44.

Slow down,
I can't see what I'm thinking.
It's probably something brilliant.
It's like a massive jigsaw puzzle.
All the pieces, thrown up in the air,
some pieces upside down
and some pieces the right side up,
showing me fragments of this brilliancy,
but I can't make out the whole picture.
I can sense it's something magnificent.
I can feel it.
One day soon, I will put it all together,
then,
then I will show you how brilliant I am.

45.

I'm running,
but I don't move an inch.
Run, run,
I'm standing still,
watching the world go by.
On the inside, I'm running,
but on the outside, you cannot see me move,
because I'm not here.

46.

Maybe I have already lost it
and this is just a movie on the inside of my eyelids.

47.

Love is like a river,
step back and see the universe within me
and without.
Without touching the river, you can not feel real love.
Love, away from the ego dictating the outcome.
Love has no outcome, love is.
The river is visible to the human eye,
but few can see it.
Step into the river with the faith of a child.
Merge yourself with the water
till there is no distinction between you and the water.
The river is everywhere,
but few can see it.

48.

Dark angel's soul,
my soul,
surrounded by holy memories of a life that once was.
I'm staring at the sky, wondering, is this it?
Am I here to just live till I die?
Have you forgotten me?
I know I have.

49.

Was I here before I was ever born?
Wondrous glorious I.

50.

The world created in your mind is not my world,
I'm not in your world.
I'm no longer in my world.
How could I?
I'm the empty space that contains it all.

51.

My soulmate is not some distant lover far away.
My soulmate is within me and without me,
being aware of my soul calling out for help,
not understanding why I'm struggling and crying.
"I am right here, and so are you," she says.
I let my guard down and let her in.
Everything vanishes. It's quiet, peaceful, silent.
I'm calm, I'm weightless, was it all a dream?
Or is this a dream?

52.

Consume everything that is not me!
Will I disappear?

53.

Silence is the only thing that makes sense.
Silence is the only thing there is.
Silence is no thing.
Silence is nothing.
Silence is everything.
Nothing makes sense.
Everything makes sense.
Silence is I.
I AM is silence.
I am silence.

54.

Eternal bliss.
Look into my illusion.
Is it convincing enough?
Have I created a good one?
Is my illusion better than yours?
All my life, I have worked on my illusion,
building, building a better one all the time.
Is it perfect now?
Just to throw it all away,
after all, it was just an illusion,
even though it was one of the best.
I don't want it anymore.
I trade my perfect illusion for nothing,
but what an amazing nothing it is.

55.

I am waiting for no one.
The days are tinted with a feeling of panic.
Panic of living, panic of not living,
panic of dying before I have fully lived,
before I have fully died.
It is time to wake up,
but the darkness is wrapping itself around me,
not letting me go.
They say it's darkest before dawn,
but can it get much darker now?
Let this be the darkest it can get.
I will do my best to stay around till the end.
Please show me the way,
show me the way home.
Teach me how to die before I die.

56.

The mind tells me so.
It must be true, the mind tells me so.
This is what I am. It must be true,
the mind tells me so.
This must be real, the mind tells me so.
Lose your mind, and reality will be revealed.
It must be true, my heart tells me so.
Lose your mind, and the truth will be revealed.
It must be true, my soul tells me so.
Stay as I AM, my soul tells me so.
I AM.

57.

Take me away from me,
let me walk alone in the midst of silence,
away from the ego's demanding voice.
I walk alone.
It's my choice to focus on the silence,
instead of the voice of the ego.
Why should I focus on something
that is of no interest to me?
A voice that doesn't want the best for me,
just the best for the ego-me.
It's doing everything for its survival.
I walk alone,
It's a place in me that speaks to me without a voice,
it speaks to me in silence,
here I can rest.
Without the voice in my head,
without attachment to illusion.
I walk alone.

58.

Remove the longing for I,
and left is only I.

59.

Autumn rain,
purifying rain,
let it wash away all illusions,
all doubts from my mind,
and leave only what is true, left for me to rest in.
The truth is obvious but hard to recognise,
when one is lost in the tumultuous world of illusion.

60.

I am the one that focuses on the mind's chatter,
and the images it shows me.
I am the one.
I am the one trying to focus on something else
in this vast universe.
I am the one.
I am the one trying to stay in my heart,
trying to find the quiet place.
I am the one.
No... I'm the one watching!

61.

Humbly I stand before you,
let me go, haven't I slaved for you long enough?
I bow down, with my head ready for decapitation,
hoping your sword is sharp.
I say goodbye and close my eyes,
when I open my eyes, you're gone,
everything is silent.

62.

Can you learn to love the feeling of falling apart,
can you accept knowing nothing,
can you stay in the quiet space?
Tell me, my friend,
what's your life without your story?

63.

My soul is calling out for help,
but no one's there.
See me,
but no one hears.
Is it all in my head,
my own private show?
Or is it my soul calling me to
wake up?

64.

Thoughts are trying to lure me into fixation,
but I'm here, I'm aware, I'm conscious.
Let them swim around me,
like sharks circling their prey,
they do not scare me anymore,
I don't have to try to flee,
I don't have to give in.
I'm here. I'm awareness,
I'm consciousness.
I'm nothing.

65.

See everything as it is,
don't let your mind distort reality.
Leave the thick fog that clouds your perception,
and stay as I am, where everything is clear.
Clouds are passing,
but everything is still so amazingly clear.

66.

Get out of the labyrinth of your own mind.
Find the way out, stay focused.
The labyrinth can help you
or lure you deeper into oblivion.
The choice is yours, and yours alone.
Are you going to take the chance this time,
or will you keep wandering around and around
till you're the only one left?
Take my hand,
take a leap of faith.
Trust me,
trust nothing.
I'm nothing,
trust me.

67.

Rain washes away my tears,
washes away the frustrating feeling of being lost.

68.

I will evoke in you what has no name,
nothing else has any meaning.
See through the big lie
that you have believed in your whole life.
Be aware! Stay! Focus!
I can feel the body grabbing onto the feeling of solidity.
Mind says I'm here,
but everything is dissolving into nothing,
not my body, just a body.
Not my feelings, just feelings.
Dissolve, dissolve.
Mind is grabbing onto memories,
not my memories, just memories.
Mind is getting desperate,
seeing everything dissolving.
Thoughts, thoughts, more thoughts,
not my thoughts, just thoughts.
Welcome me when I say goodbye.
Dissolving into nothing.
Mind screams out loud,
but no sound is coming out of nothing.

69.

Stay silent outside the prison of your ego,
be aware of the turmoil inside the prison gates.
The gates are locked,
but you've got the key,
the key is silence,
the key is awareness,
the key is consciousness,
nothing can keep you imprisoned,
just realise that you *are* silence,
you are awareness, you are consciousness.
There is no prison, there is no key, there is no self,
there is no me.

70.

Is this it?
Will I be stuck here forever and ever,
or am I the one,
the one watching it all play out in front of me?
Give me strength to ignore the mind's
persistent talk.
The silence is so vast,
why focus on the chatter,
when everything around the chatter is total silence?
Silence.
Vast, empty space,
nothing,
void.
I want to move away from the mind,
but it sucks me in again and again,
like a whirlpool.
I can see it all,
but still, I get entangled in the nonsense of the mind.
It's got so much to say,
so much to show,
so much that I can't possibly manage to ignore.
Focus on the silence,
beautiful silence.
I'm in the silence,
I am the silence,
no want,
I am.

71.

Beautiful, beautiful being.
Being beautiful, being human.
Human being.

72.

Have I lost this battle?
Am I still a worthy worrier,
even though it seems like a never-ending war?
The war is between my mind
and the truth of what I am.
It's a one-sided war that can not be won
until I lay down my weapons and realise
that we are on the same side.
My war is in my head,
and as long as the fighting is going on,
there will be no peace.
Truth is my ally.
Truth is within me.
Truth is me.
I am truth,
I'm silence,
I'm the silent warrior for peace.

73.

Colour and light
playing seriously on the canvas,
making stunning pictures.
Breathtaking,
wondrous, silent,
wordless signs, leading to your inner self.
Feel.
The painter has given you a key to your own universe.
It brings you silence
in the midst of your tumultuous world.
The world is full of signposts,
find them,
take them in.
Cherish them,
breathe in the moment.
Naked,
vulnerable,
fearless, silent.
You are here to meet the I.

74.

Running away from time, run, run!
You can't find me where you are looking.
You can know me, but you can not find me.
Stop looking.
We are one!
You're like a dog chasing your own tail.
I'm here,
I am always here.
Stop doing.
To do is futile.
Just be still.
Stillness is what you are.

75.

Floating around in empty space,
moving into different illusions,
different alluring, amazing worlds.
Now I set anchor outside the dream state,
just visiting the illusionary world,
without being swept away.
I know my way home,
I'm no longer lost,
in the matrix of the mind.

76.

I've been chasing myself my whole life,
like chasing my own shadow.
When I finally stopped,
I managed to catch up with myself,
realising that,
I've been here the whole time.

77.

No past is here,
past this threshold, it is no more.
No thoughts can enter here,
thoughts stay out there,
no risk of getting enticed by the mind, or?
Be vigilant!
Peace, quiet, silence.
I am silence.
This is not a place to stay in,
this is what I am.
I am.
I'm empty space,
nothing can touch me,
still, everything can move in me,
and nothing can exist without me.
I am everything,
but I'm no thing.
I am nothing,
I am.

78.

Snow, pure snow, cover me,
make me as pure as you.
Freeze all the clinging to thought,
make it fragile and break it.
Break all attachment to my false identity,
like breaking fine crystal.
Make it shatter into a million pieces,
and melt into the ground of oblivion.

79.

I walk through the valley of confusion,
sleepwalking through life.
The only place I have really visited is my own head,
lost in the mind's confusing model of what it calls life.
I finally realise,
this is not life.
I have to get out of this prison
before the walls get too high to climb over,
but no action is really needed,
no action is the key.
But I rather climb, knowing I'm getting closer,
the mind says.
Mind is very helpful,
like a bad friend with ulterior motives.
I linger a little bit longer,
then I let go of the helping hand of the mind.
Walking up the hill where clarity exists,
here the view is so much better.
It's time to live outside the prison walls.
It's clear to me now,
there never was a prison,
never was a prison wall,
the mind is a tool,
not a prison.

80.

I'm running, running, running.
I can't stop running.
My mind is galloping like a crazy rabbit,
caught in the headlights of a car,
racing down the highway.
Run, run.

81.

How many times do I have to shed my skin,
just to find another layer of identity?
Endlessly recreating an illusory self,
why can't this just stop,
now, here, in this lifetime?
No more rebuilding,
I have had enough.
I shed another layer,
and, nothing,
there is nothing,
I am nothing.
No more layers.
No more identities.
Nothing more to build on.
Nothing, nothing,
except, all the nothing that I am.

82.

You are already free,
just hold on to I,
hold on as if nothing is real.
Nothing *is* real, in this world of illusion.
It separates us
into a multitude that does not exist.
Hold on to I.
Stay, stay, stay.
You're here, no need to be anywhere else.
It's all just a very captivating illusion,
relax, and see it for what it is.
You're not bound to duality,
not bound to suffering,
not bound to this illusionary world.
Come with me, stay with me,
stay, stay with I.
Let's stay here in the space of no borders,
no fear.
The space of no self, no boundaries.
The no space of nothing, and everything,
nowhere and everywhere.
It's only I,
but it's the most glorious I, you can ever imagine,
it's the I that contains everything.

83.

The mind is pulling me in the wrong direction,
any direction that will not lead me to what I am.
The mind gives me promises of a better future.
How can you promise me something
that you do not have any control over?
The only way you can promise me a better future
is to let me go.
You're not the saviour you pretend to be.
You're not my friend.
If you're my friend, you should let me go.
If you're my friend, you should let me be.
But you're not my friend,
you're not even real.

84.

Take me away from me.
Rest is near.
Struggle no more to be who you already are.
The pain has to stop.
Walk with me, hold my hand.
I feel the earth breathing through me like a hurt child.
Blossom, my friend,
wipe away all your tears.
Breathe, breathe,
you can't stop now!
Stay with me,
stay till the end of time,
caress me, hold me.
I'm slipping away, or is it you?
I'm slipping away from myself.
There's nowhere to go, no one to be.
Be with me in this darkest hour.
Light is no more.
Wake up!
Darkness is no more.
No more darkness visible to I.
No more pain.
Stay.
Be.
No more pain.
Be,
Awake.

85.

Don't go out there to events and thoughts.
Stay right here in my arms,
relax, you're home.

86.

I'm a free being,
being captured in my own mind.
In bondage by believing in what's not true.
I'm a free being. Truth is what I am.
I'm a free being,
being trapped in this world of illusions.
I'm a free being.
I walk alone, I walk in my own footsteps,
circling round and round
till I get too dizzy to think clearly.
I know I am free, help me to remember.
I'm a free being,
being oblivious of my own freedom.
I stand tall,
I have both feet firmly on the ground,
steady and determined to be grounded in the truth.
I'm a free being,
I walk alone.
I walk till I reach the edge of this world.
One more step
and this illusion no longer has a grip on me.
I AM a free being.
I AM FREE.

87.

My soul hungers for solutions
to this dilemma I call life.
Stop pulling me into your domain.
This sleep is like a punishment
for something I have done,
or is it for something I haven't done,
or is it just a wicked game?
Maybe one day,
I will wake up and see it was just a game,
a game of delusion.
"Relax and be, be nothing."
Everything is so vast.
Why do I still get sucked into this black hole
of the mind?
"Stay here, don't go out, just be."
I'm moving turbulently through space,
bumping into every thought that shows up.
Every emotion gets me spinning out of control.
I try to see what's in front of me,
I try to feel what's around me.
I stay, but I can't stay.
I move without moving.
I move through space like a ship out of control,
sucked into empty space,
which is not empty at all.
I'm bumping into meaningless memories.
Sucked into another black hole,
where did I go?
How long was I gone?
Back on track, or?

No control.
No control at all.
"Relax. Swim like a fish in endless clear water."
But the water is not clear.
It's polluted.
Polluted by memories, thoughts and emotions,
coming from nowhere,
going nowhere.
"Just watch."
Back to square one,
back to the beginning.
The beginning of time as I know it.
"Feel, see, sense."
Uncontrollably lost in the labyrinth again.
This is not the first time.
*"The middle is no more the end than the beginning.
Get back to the beginning."*
I move, but I don't move.
I'm lost in the illusion of time and space,
lost in thoughts and memories.
Time does not exist, and neither do I,
the made-up person with all its memories
and emotions, does not exist.
*"Be still and listen to no sound,
see no thing, feel the emptiness of all illusions."*
The empty space is me.
Everything else is an illusion.

88.

I'm here,
I am.
Why continue this oscillation back and forth?
I'm here.
I'm ready.
I am, already.
I'm already here!

89.

Seek inside, and you shall find.
The truth is leading you.
The sky, the moon, the stars are guiding you.
Can you accept what you have found?

90.

I open the door into my inner self
and discover there is no self here.
What am I?
No self, no separate world,
no war, no disagreement,
no fighting, no thing.
Nothing.

91.

I can see the beauty of the self,
I can see the ugliness of the self,
I can see the pain of the self.
Why would the self care?
It doesn't exist.
I'm pain, I'm ugly, I'm beautiful.
I'm not pain, I'm not ugly, I'm not beautiful,
I'm the one watching it all unfold in front of me.

92.

I feel like I'm balancing
on a slackline between two worlds.
I keep falling off into the mind and all its confusion.

93.

How can we learn the wonder of now,
when we never stay still?
Walk with me.
Don't linger in the past or the future,
it's just a story, the fiction of your mind.
Stay with me,
in this silent, spacious moment of no time.
Don't see, don't sense, just know, just be.
We are here,
always here and always now.

94.

No time is more valuable than no time.
It's only now.

95.

Despair not.
Weightless, I fly through the air,
over this turbulent world looking for silence.
I'm here not knowing which way to go
to find peace from the mind,
to find peace for this restless body.
I desperately try to navigate through life.
It's too confusing.
I try to distance myself from the fog that surrounds me.
I fly above, there is less fog,
I can breathe for a moment,
I try to fly below the fog, I feel confused and scared,
till I finally remember the one and only truth,
the one and only reality.
There is no fog,
there is no body,
there is no me.
It's all a confusing dream,
it's all an illusion.

96.

I need to remember how it is to be alive.

97.

Show me how to move around in this world
without feeling hurt,
without feeling overwhelmed.
Everything is too much, and nothing is enough.
I'm a warrior fighting for survival.
I'm gasping for air,
trying not to suffocate
from all the thoughts and emotions.
I'm being pushed and pulled by the mind.
I turn around and walk away.
I can not stay.
I do not belong.
How can one feel too much and yet feel nothing?

98.

Walking barefoot through life,
seeking safety in the illusion created by the mind.

99.

Put me together, I have fallen apart,
I'm spread all over the world.
One enlightened being after another
will put me together again.
I will be whole.
One big soul, reunited after the big bang.

100.

I'm empty inside,
but I still talk to you, something is.
I cry on the inside,
but on the outside, you can see me interact and smile.
You can't see it, but I'm balancing on a thin thread,
sometimes I tip over and lose it,
but with strong meaningless determination,
I catch my balance again.
I don't think you notice,
you're too occupied being you.
If you could see it, would you be impressed?
The balancing game.
At times it's the only thing I can do,
just trying to keep my balance.
You can't see it, but I'm not even here anymore.
I'm lost. I can't find myself.
Maybe one day, I'll willingly lose my balance
and let go of the thin thread
that seems to keep me sane.
Maybe the thread is the insanity,
and without it, I would be whole.

101.

It's all one.
Slow down,
and you will see what is invisible to the human eye,
ungraspable to the human mind.
Slow down,
It's all one.

102.

Be aware of the one that hears,
be aware of the one that sees,
be aware of the one that is thinking.
Be aware.

103.

Bit by bit, I fall away,
nothing will be left,
nothing is always here.
Nothing was here before you came along,
and nothing will be here
when you finally leave me alone.
Here is nothing talking to nothing.

104.

One day I will not be here,
but I will be more present than ever.
One day you will see me for what I am,
Nothing!

105.

Seeking, seeking, seeking!
"Stay focused, I'm here!"
Thoughts are floating around in the air like fog.
No way to get around them.
No way to duck,
no way to walk through this fog
without getting totally soaked from top to toe.
There must be a way to ignore them.
"Focus, my friend."
I'm here,
the thoughts are there.
I'm here.
What am I?
I'm here.
I am.
It's like being inside a tornado.
Thoughts, feelings,
emotions, images,
sounds are all sucking me in.
If I could just make it to the centre,
then everything would be calm.
"Stay focused."
I'm watching it all moving all around me.
It's out there,
it's someone else's nightmare,
it's no one's nightmare.
I'm here,
I'm still,
I'm stillness,
I am.

106.

I'm lost, to be found.
Find me.
Have I really been lost all this time,
or have I been dreaming?
I'm here, I'm awake.
Life is.
Life is not what I thought.
Life is not a thought.
You have been my enemy and my friend.
Enemy when I thought you were my friend,
and a friend when I thought you were my enemy.
Life is. I am.
Everything else is an illusion.
Lost, never to be found again.

107.

My world is on fire.
Let it burn, burn till I can feel nothing.
But nothing is not a feeling.
It just is.

108.

What can I do if I fade away,
away from me, from I.
Is it happening all over again,
or is it happening for the first time?
Have I been here before?
It seems so,
but this time, it's different,
it's more silent, more clear.
I can see a distance between us,
or can I feel it?
No need to think.
I'm here.
Waiting to get lost again.
But I'm still here,
not waiting,
just being here,
not lost,
being totally home.

109.

Be a stargazer,
not a cloud chaser.
Let it all be.
You're the creator.
Not the seeker.

110.

Metamorphosis,
I can feel it.
One day you will not recognise me.
I go back and forth,
shredding my skin,
almost getting out of this cocoon,
out of the life I have made up in my head,
my own personal "reality".
There is nothing real about this reality.
Metamorphosis is near.
I will finally lose this suffocating cocoon,
get out, and spread my wings.
Why would I choose to stay and get confused
every time my mind inserts its claws into me?
Stuck in the web of my own creation,
I AM getting out,
out of reach from the claws of the mind.
Time to undergo metamorphosis.

111.

Life is a poem, not yet read.
Silence is the answer to all the questions
never asked.

Just let go, I've got you.